PARIS

TRAVEL GUIDE

The Ultimate Pocket Guide to the City of Love:
Unlock the Charm and Hidden Gems of the City.
Everything you Need to Know Before Plan a Trip to
Paris

STUART HARTLEY

TABLE OF CONTENTS

INTRODUCTION

Numerous people worldwide flock to Paris yearly. The French capital and a key economic and political centre in Paris, Paris attracts almost as many visitors as London does among European cities. This book will inform you where to stay, how to travel around the city, and how to save money while you're there.

Paris is stunning at any time of year, whether the height of summer and the banks of Canal St. Martin are buzzing with activity when the Eiffel Tower seems to penetrate dark storm clouds. May through June and September through November offer pleasant temperatures and fewer tourists than the summer months.

Taking a trip during the week rather than on weekends or holidays will help you save money. Mondays and Tuesdays are off-limits for museum visitors.

You can take advantage of the low-cost airlines serving the city from other European cities or fly directly into the city from several other locations. You should take your kids to Disneyland as a complete and total surprise if you have any.

Paris has over 100 restaurants awarded the Michelin star, and it is home to more museums and galleries than any other city in the world.

Planning your trip to this one-of-a-kind city will be easier if you learn about its fascinating past and gain familiarity with the city of Paris.

When you know the greatest places to visit, the museums you can't miss, where to stay, and what to eat in one of the world's most romantic cities, get ready to experience one of the world's most alluring locations and pack your bags.

This book will help you make the most of your time in Paris, whether it's your first time there or your fifty-first.

Let's get started!

CHAPTER 1: NAVIGATING THE CITY'S TRANSPORTATION SYSTEM

Paris has an extensive public transportation system that includes the metro, buses, trams, RER trains, and a bike-sharing program. Navigating the transportation system in Paris can be overwhelming at first, but once you understand how it works, it's easy to get around.

Instead of taking taxis or tourist buses, try getting around like a local by taking the metro, bus, or bike. Because of this, you'll have a new perspective on the city and the chance to mingle with the people.

Paris is served by four different tram routes that travel throughout the city's outskirts. You may use the same metro, RER, and bus fare card.

The one-way fare on the airport RoissyBus to Paris-Charles de Gaulle (CDG) is €12. Depending on the bus you take and where in Paris you're headed, the fare to Paris-Orly (ORY) might range from €9.50 to €12.10.

Communal bicycles are available through the Velib program in the French capital of Paris. Single rides cost 3 EUR, day passes cost 5, and a 3-day pass may be purchased for 20 EUR. Ten Euros will get you a day's use of electric bikes.

To travel around Paris, many people have used e-scooters or electric scooters. Many firms, including Lime and Tier, provide scooters at the same basic price—around 1 EUR to unlock it, plus another.15-.20 EUR per minute.

Costly Taxis in the City (rides cost a minimum of 7.10 EUR regardless of where you are going). Even when the subway is open late, there is no reason to ride it. Do your best to stay away from them.

The excellent public transit system in Paris makes using Uber essentially superfluous.

Renting a car in Paris is bad because driving there is difficult for everyone. Do not get a rental car here; you won't require one because getting out of town is as simple and inexpensive as taking the bus or train.

Here are some tips for navigating Paris's transportation system:

Use the metro: The metro is the fastest and most convenient way around Paris and the surrounding suburbs. There are 16 metro lines, from around 5:30 am until approximately 1:15 am, with some lines running until 1 am on Fridays and Saturdays.

Each line has a different colour and number, so knowing which line you need to take is important.

You can buy single tickets or a rechargeable Navigo pass, which gives you unlimited travel for a week or a month.

You can purchase single tickets or a multi-day pass, and taxis and ride-sharing services like Uber are also available.

Take the bus: The bus is another option for getting around Paris. It's slower than the metro, but it can be more scenic and allows you to see more of the city. You can buy single tickets or a rechargeable Navigo pass, which also works on the bus.

Paris has a comprehensive bus network that serves all parts of the city, including night buses that operate during the hours when the metro is closed. Some buses are equipped with free Wi-Fi, and most buses have dedicated lanes, which makes them faster than cars during peak hours.

Trams: Paris has four tramway lines on the city's outskirts. These are great options for commuting to the suburbs, as they connect with the metro and RER trains.

Try the RER: The RER (Réseau Express Régional) is a rapid transit system that serves the Parisian suburbs and beyond. It's a great option for reaching destinations like Versailles or Disneyland Paris. The RER has five lines that run through Paris, and trains are generally faster than the metro.

The RER is a suburban train system that connects Paris to its suburbs. You can buy single tickets or a rechargeable Navigo pass, which also works on the RER.

Use a bike: Paris has a bike-sharing system called Vélib', a great option for short trips around the city. You can rent a bike from any Vélib station and return it to any other station. You can buy a 24-hour pass or a long-term subscription. You can rent a bike for 30 minutes or more and return it to any Vélib station.

Walk: Paris's best sights can be reached on foot, making the city ideal for strolling. A person can see more of the city and gain some exercise by walking around.

Using these different transportation modes, you can easily get around Paris. The metro is the fastest and most convenient way to travel within the city, while buses, trams, and RER trains are great options if you travel to the suburbs or other parts of the region. The bike-sharing program is a fun and eco-friendly way to explore Paris.

TIPS FOR BUYING AND USING METRO AND BUS TICKETS

The metro and buses generally run from 5:30 am to midnight, with some lines running later on Fridays and Saturdays. Check the schedule to ensure you can catch the last train or bus.

The fare for a ride on the city's extensive metro system is only €2.10, and the system is quite easy to navigate. You must use cash or a reloadable Navigo card (€5) to avoid lines since contactless payments aren't accepted.

You can purchase tickets for the Metro, bus, tram, and train at ticket vending machines in Metro stations, bus stops, and train stations. You can also buy tickets online or via a mobile app. Single tickets cost €1.90 and can be used for one journey on any mode of transportation.

You can use the RATP (Régie Autonome des Transports Parisiens) website or mobile app to plan your route. Enter your starting point and destination, and the app will give you the best route and estimated travel time.

Here are some tips for buying and using metro and bus tickets in Paris:

Buy a carnet of tickets: A carnet is a book of 10 metro or bus tickets cheaper than buying single tickets. You can buy a carnet at any metro station, bus stop, or tabac (tobacco shop).

Consider a day pass: If you plan on using public transportation frequently in one day, consider buying a day pass, which gives you unlimited travel. You can buy a day pass at any metro station, bus stop, or tabac.

The Paris Visite Pass is a good option for tourists, as it offers unlimited travel on public transportation for a set period (1-5 days). The Navigo Pass is a weekly or monthly pass for residents or frequent visitors.

Choose the right ticket: Make sure you buy the right ticket for your journey. Different ticket prices depend on the number of zones you'll be travelling in. If you're staying in central Paris, you'll only need a ticket for zones 1-2.

Validate your ticket: Before you board the metro or bus, make sure to validate your ticket in the machines located at the entrance to the metro station or the front of the bus. You could face a fine if you're caught without a validated ticket.

Look for the yellow machines at Metro stations or on buses and trams. Hold your ticket against the machine, which will stamp the date and time.

Hold onto your ticket: Keep your ticket with you at all times while travelling, as you may be asked to show it by a ticket inspector.

Use the Navigo pass: If you are in Paris for a week or longer, consider getting a Navigo pass, which gives you unlimited travel on public transportation for a week or a month. You can buy a Navigo pass at any metro station or RATP office.

Watch out for pickpockets: Remember where you are, and don't lose your stuff. Especially in crowded areas like metro stations and buses, pickpockets can be active.

Be aware of strikes: Strikes are common in France and can disrupt public transportation. Check the RATP website or social media accounts for information about strikes and any changes to the schedule.

Following these tips, you can easily buy and use metro and bus tickets in Paris and avoid potential problems.

HOW TO NAVIGATE THE CITY ON FOOT OR BY BIKE

Paris is a great city to explore on foot or by bike. You will walk one of the world's most recognizable streets, from the Arc de Triomphe to the Louvre. Plenty of high-end stores and restaurants along its bustling streets make it an ideal location for daytime and evening club hopping and retail therapy. Visit in the wee hours of the morning to find the place empty. It's a fantastic photo opportunity.

Exploring new areas on foot is great fun, popping into stores and museums as you go. An ideal stroll is seeing the Marais and stopping for tea at Mariage Freres in the middle of the day. It's the cutest place ever, and they serve the world's finest teas (and pastries!).

When the weather is nice, you can stroll along Canal Saint-Martin. Go to Ten Belles for a cappuccino, and if you become hungry, try one of Du Pain et des Idées' outstanding escargot pastries. Along the way, you're bound to find some additional charming establishments.

The enchanted Le Bristol Spa may be found high above the rooftops of Paris. With its teak decking and surrounding windows, the famed rooftop pool is reminiscent of a yacht's interior and provides a stunning panorama of Sacré Coeur and the Eiffel Tower. The best method to see everything you missed while walking!

To help you get around the city, we have compiled some useful information about the following transit options:

Use a map or a GPS: Before you set out on your walk or bike ride, ensure you have a good map or GPS device. You can find free maps at most tourist offices; many hotels also provide maps to guests.

Use a bike-sharing program: Paris has a bike-sharing program called Vélib', which allows you to rent a bike from one of the automated stations throughout the city. This is a convenient and affordable way to explore Paris by bike. You can rent a bike for 30 minutes or more and return it to any Vélib station.

Plan your route: Before you start your walk or bike ride, plan your route. Consider using bike lanes or pedestrian areas to avoid busy streets and intersections.

Be aware of traffic rules: If you're biking, follow the traffic rules and signs. In Paris, bikes must follow the same traffic laws as cars, including stopping at red lights and riding on the right side of the road.

Stay hydrated: Paris can get hot during summer, so stay hydrated while walking or biking. Bring a water bottle with you, or stop at one of the many cafes or fountains throughout the city to refill your bottle.

Wear comfortable shoes or clothes: If you plan to walk a lot, wear comfortable shoes suitable for walking long distances. If you're biking, wear comfortable clothes that won't get caught in the bike's gears.

Watch out for pickpockets: Pay attention to where you are and don't lose your stuff., especially in crowded areas where pickpockets can be active.

Following these tips, you can navigate Paris on foot or by bike and enjoy all the city offers while staying safe and comfortable.

CHAPTER 2: EXPLORING NEIGHBORHOODS OFF THE BEATEN PATH

Paris has a lot of touristy activities and experiences, but there are also many unique and off-the-beaten-path things to do.

Numerous distinct arrondissements make up the city of Paris. While it's worthwhile to check out the city's most well-known attractions, travellers should also try to discover the area's less-trodden neighbourhoods.

When visiting Paris, exploring the various neighbourhoods is important, each offering something unique.

Montmartre is a great place to go if you're looking for an artistic atmosphere, Le Marais is great for its ancient building, and Saint-Germain-des-Prés is great for its trendy shops and cafes.

Here are some tips for exploring neighbourhoods off the beaten path in Paris:

Take a walking tour: Consider taking a walking tour of some of the lesser-known neighbourhoods in Paris. This is a great way to discover hidden gems and understand the local culture.

Explore on foot or bike: One of the best ways to explore off-the-beaten-path neighbourhoods is simply walking or cycling through them. This lets you see things you might miss if you travel by car or public transportation.

Visit local markets: Paris is home to many local markets, which are great places to discover the local culture and meet locals. Check out the Marché des Enfants Rouges in the Marais, or the Marché d'Aligre in the 12th arrondissement.

Try local cuisine: Each neighbourhood in Paris has its unique food scene. Try visiting local restaurants or cafes to taste the neighbourhood's cuisine.

Visit small museums or galleries: Paris has many small museums and galleries, often featuring local artists or lesser-known works. Check out the Musée de la Chasse et de la Nature in the Marais, or the Musée Gustave Moreau in the 9th arrondissement.

Attend local events: Watch for local events like street festivals, live music performances, or outdoor markets. These events are a great way to experience the local culture and meet locals.

By following these tips, you can discover some of the lesser-known neighbourhoods in Paris and uniquely experience the local culture.

OVERVIEW OF LESSER-KNOWN PARISIAN NEIGHBOURHOODS

Paris has many unique neighbourhoods, each with its character and charm. Here are some of the more interesting but less well-known areas in Paris:

Canal Saint-Martin: This neighbourhood, located in the 10th and 11th arrondissements, is known for its picturesque canal and charming cafes and shops. Enjoy a glass of wine or coffee while watching the boats go by at this waterfront cafe.

Belleville: Located in the 20th arrondissement, Belleville is a diverse and lively neighbourhood known for its street art, multicultural food scene, and panoramic city views.

Butte-aux-Cailles: This charming neighbourhood, located in the 13th arrondissement, is known for its narrow streets, colourful murals, and lively bar and restaurant scene.

Batignolles: This neighbourhood, located in the 17th arrondissement, is a quieter and more residential area known for its leafy parks, trendy boutiques, and artisanal food shops.

Oberkampf: This lively neighbourhood, located in the 11th arrondissement, is known for its vibrant nightlife scene, street art, and eclectic mix of cafes and bars.

Montmartre: Since the Belle Époque of the 19th century, Montmartre has been a haven for hungry artists. The district is known for its beautiful perspective of Paris, artistic cafés and bars, charming cobblestone streets, and the city's lone winery (Vignes du Clos Montmartre).

Even though some of its former splendour has been lost, it is still one of Paris' trendier neighbourhoods. It's perfect for history buffs and anybody interested in Hemingway's and Stein's haunts. At the hill's peak stands Sacré-Coeur, a basilica widely recognized as a city symbol. Take in the sunset from atop the steps or the sloping lawn. Visits to the basilica are entirely free of charge.

Passy: This upscale neighbourhood, located in the 16th arrondissement, is known for its elegant Haussmannian architecture, designer boutiques, and stunning views of the Eiffel Tower.

Père-Lachaise: This neighbourhood, located in the 20th arrondissement, is known for its famous cemetery, the final resting place of many famous figures, including Jim Morrison, Edith Piaf, and Oscar Wilde.

Exploring these and other lesser-known neighbourhoods in Paris allows you to discover a different side of the city and uniquely experience the local culture.

RECOMMENDATIONS FOR LOCAL MARKETS, RESTAURANTS, AND SHOPS

It's understandable to want to experience the local culture when travelling to a new place rather than just feeling like a tourist. Consider staying in a local neighbourhood rather than a touristy area. This will allow you to experience the local way of life, shop at local markets, and eat at neighbourhood cafes and restaurants.

Paris is home to many bustling markets that offer a glimpse into daily life in the city.

Here are some recommendations for local markets, restaurants, and shops in Paris:

LOCAL MARKETS:

Marché des Enfants Rouges: This market, located in the Marais, is the oldest covered market in Paris and features a variety of vendors selling fresh produce, cheese, and prepared foods.

Marché d'Aligre: This market, located in the 12th arrondissement, is a bustling open-air market with vendors selling fresh produce, meat, cheese, and other local specialities.

The diverse street food vendors at **Marché Saint-Quentin** (less than ten minutes walk from Gare du Nord) sell great local produce and are convenient for Eurostar travellers.

Les Puces de Paris Saint-Ouen is the largest flea market in the world, drawing bargain hunters on Friday mornings and for the whole weekend and into Monday.

RESTAURANTS:

Visit **Babka Zana in Montmartre** for a quick bite to eat on the run. Dessert babka flavours like pistachio and tangerine make a classic sandwich like a croque monsieur seem boring.

Join the all-black hipster crowd at **Paperboy** Paris in the Latin Quarter if you crave a Frenchie sandwich. Cafeteria-style seating, top-notch caffeine delivery, and abundant healthy plant-based selections.

L'As du Fallafel: This popular falafel stands in the Marais and is known for its delicious and affordable sandwiches.

Le Comptoir du Relais: This cosy restaurant in the Saint-Germain-des-Prés neighbourhood serves classic French dishes made with local ingredients.

Miznon: This Israeli street food restaurant in the Marais is known for its tasty pita sandwiches and creative vegetable dishes.

Chez Nous in the 6ème is a classic wine bar that won't break the bank and features truffle-scented cheese plates, warm, casual service, and a convivial atmosphere. The wine on the wine list is available for complimentary pours at the (little) community tables.

Le Perchoir Ménilmontant is the place to be (Wednesday through Saturday) if you want cocktails and a view of Paris. In terms of atmosphere, it's hard to top the seventh story of an industrial building that hosts frequent live music events. Le Perchoir also operates bar restaurants in Le Marais and Porte de Versailles.

Le Piano Vache is a low-key Latin Quarter dance club open Monday through Saturday (closed on Sundays). Inexpensive (by Parisian standards) pints can be found in this always-packed and ever-so-slightly-dirty watering hole that hosts jazz evenings on the regular.

SHOPS:

Merci: This trendy concept store, located in the Marais, features a mix of fashion, home decor, and accessories from local and international designers.

Visit the three-story Merci for a wide selection of home goods, unique clothing, and a fantastic used bookstore-cum-café. There are outfits made out of bath towels that are marked down to a steal from the original price of €200 if you look at the label carefully before you buy.

La Trésorerie: This beautiful shop, located in the 10th arrondissement, sells a carefully curated selection of home goods, kitchenware, and textiles.

Le Labo: This perfume shop in the Marais and Saint-Germain-des-Prés sells a range of high-end fragrances made with natural ingredients.

Stop by the vegan concept store and café Aujourd'hui Demain for one-of-a-kind apparel, prints, and organic fare.

By visiting these and other local markets, restaurants, and shops in Paris, you can experience the city like a local and discover unique products and flavours you won't find in tourist areas.

CHAPTER 3: DECIDING WHICH ATTRACTIONS TO PRIORITIZE

As a tourist destination, Paris seems tailor-made. Tourists are drawn back to the city time and time again by its inviting streets, squares, buildings, gardens, and monuments.

Trips to the Eiffel Tower, the Louvre Museum, the Sacré-Cœur Basilica, the Champs-Élysées and Notre Dame Cathedral are among the most iconic experiences in the City of Lights.

One must not leave Paris without seeing a performance at the world-famous Moulin Rouge cabaret, taking a stroll around one of the city's most beautiful areas like Montmartre, or visiting the top of the Montparnasse Tower after dark. Also, visit the Seine River and the many beautiful parks, gardens, and squares.

With so many amazing attractions and activities in Paris, deciding which ones to prioritize can be challenging.

Paris has so many attractions and neighbourhoods to explore that it can be difficult to decide where to prioritize your limited time.

The following advice will help you make the most of your time and select the most appropriate attractions based on your interests:

Create a list of must-see attractions: Before arriving in Paris, list the attractions you absolutely must see. This can include iconic landmarks like the Eiffel Tower and Notre Dame and museums, galleries, and other cultural institutions that interest you.

Consider your interests: Think about the types of activities and attractions that you enjoy most. For example, if you're a foodie, you might prioritize visiting local markets and restaurants. If you're interested in history, you might focus on museums and historical sites.

Check the opening hours: Before visiting an attraction, check its opening hours to ensure they fit your schedule. Some attractions, like museums, may have limited hours on certain days, so planning is important.

Consider the season and weather: Some attractions may be more enjoyable during certain seasons or weather conditions. For example, visiting the outdoor markets or gardens might be more pleasant on a sunny day, while indoor museums and galleries are perfect for a rainy day.

Don't try to do too much: Paris offers so much that seeing everything in one trip can be tempting. However, this can be overwhelming and exhausting. Instead, focus on key attractions and neighbourhoods and allow yourself time to enjoy them.

Using these tips, you can prioritize the most important attractions to you and make the most of your time in Paris.

OVERVIEW OF PARIS' MOST POPULAR ATTRACTIONS AND LANDMARKS

Paris has many iconic attractions and landmarks popular with locals and tourists. Here are some of the most popular:

Eiffel Tower: Eiffel Tower is one of Paris's most recognizable symbols. The tower stood at 300 meters and was originally constructed for the 1889 Universal Exhibition. Take the lift to the observation deck for a bird's-eye view of the city below.

Go there early to avoid the crowds and visit the peak. Depending on the date, ticket prices are between 16 and 26 Euros. In addition, for 52 Euros, you can ride an elevator straight to the top. Picnicking and picture-taking on the grassy Champ Mars in front of it is a must.

Louvre Museum: Over 35,000 works of art are on show at the Louvre, making it one of the world's largest and most renowned museums. Several famous works of art may be discovered there, including the Mona Lisa and the Winged Victory of Samothrace, to name just two of them.

The Louvre has thousands of square feet of exhibit space, and the museum has millions of artefacts and works of art (including the Mona Lisa and the Venus de Milo).

You'll need at least two full days to take it all in, but the highlights may be seen in a single afternoon. Timed skip-the-line tickets can be purchased for an extra 17 EUR, and general admission is 17 EUR. The museum is open until 11 p.m. on Wednesdays, making it a great choice if you want to dodge the crowd. Around 7 o'clock, it empties.

Notre-Dame Cathedral: A gothic masterpiece, Notre Dame Cathedral stands on the Île de la Cité in the middle of Paris. It's famous for stunning stained glass windows, rose windows, and gargoyles.

The Gothic marvel, the Notre Dame Cathedral in Paris, was built between 1163 and 1334. To better appreciate the stonework and a closer look at the Gallery of Chimeras, the amazing birds and monsters watching over the balustrade climb from the north tower to the south. The exterior has been renovated in recent years, but the interior still retains some of the charming grime of its Gothic past. Ten Euros are required to ascend the tower. The 2019 fire has forced the closure of Notre Dame Cathedral.

The Latin Quarter: The Latin Quarter is a historical district close to Notre Dame Cathedral. It is characterized by narrow, winding lanes that branch off at odd angles and eventually open into quaint, cafe-lined squares. A wide variety of dining options, watering holes, and jazz clubs can be found in this area.

The Pantheon: Built as a church in the Neoclassical style, this Latin Quarter structure now serves as a national cemetery for notable French citizens such as Marie Curie, Victor Hugo, Jean-Jacques Rousseau, Louis Braille, and Voltaire. The cost of entry is 11.50 euros.

Champs-Élysées: One of the most recognizable streets in all of Paris, the Champs-Élysées is home to a wide variety of restaurants, cafes, and theatres. It's a popular spot for tourists and locals alike and is especially beautiful at night when the lights illuminate the trees.

Arc de Triomphe: Another well-known structure in Paris is the Arc de Triomphe. The structure dated back to 1806 and was erected as a memorial to the French soldiers who had fallen in the Napoleonic Wars. Tourists that make the ascent will be rewarded with panoramic vistas of the metropolis below.

This structure dominates Place Charles de Gaulle. Dedicated to the memory of those who fell in the wars against the French during the Revolution and Napoleon's Empire. Tourists can pay 13 EUR to ascend the Arc's 284 steps and get a bird's-eye view of the city and a brief history lesson.

Sacré-Cœur: The Sacré-Cœur is a stunning basilica located on the hill of Montmartre. It's famous for its white dome and stunning views of the city.

The Sacré-Coeur (free entry, open every day) is probably more impressive than Notre Dame (currently recovering from the 2019 fire and closed to the public), and the views from the basilica steps are among the best in Paris.

Palace of Versailles: Some of the world's most extravagant cathedrals and palaces were constructed in Paris before the French decapitated their rulers and prohibited religious symbols.

The Palace of Versailles is stunning just outside Paris. It was the home of French kings and queens for over a century and is famous for its opulent décor and stunning gardens.

The mind is boggled by the 2,300 rooms and hall of mirrors at the Château de Versailles (€21.50, closed on Mondays).

The Victor Hugo House: Beautiful apartment built in 1605. Victor Hugo, the author of Les Misérables and The Hunchback of Notre Dame, settled there at 30 and became its most renowned resident. A museum honouring his life and works is housed in his former home. Even though it's on the small side, the museum packs a lot of punch for Hugo fans like myself. His entire life, from childhood to death, is represented in this house through themed rooms. It doesn't cost anything to get in.

Catacombs of Paris: Paris rests on a network of tunnels dug out for mining purposes centuries ago. The French resistance utilized these tunnels during World War II, and later in the 1990s, they became popular places to hold raves. The Catacombs of Paris, an ossuary containing the remains of more than 6 million Parisians, can be found within this network of tunnels.

In the 18th century, this cemetery was established because of public health worries about crowded cemeteries. It's one of the city's most unusual and fascinating attractions. Last-minute tickets, if available, can be purchased for 14 EUR.

Holocaust Memorial: The Mémorial de la Shoah's great display on France, anti-Semitism and the Holocaust rarely sees many visitors. It's a tremendous bummer because this site has excellent resources and detailed information, and it doesn't cost anything to get in.

You'll taste Paris's rich history, art, and culture by visiting these attractions and landmarks.

TIPS FOR AVOIDING LONG LINES AND CROWDS

Paris is a popular tourist destination, so many attractions can get crowded, especially during the peak travel season. However, there are a few tips you can follow to avoid long lines and crowds:

Plan: Before arriving in Paris, list the attractions you want to visit and plan your itinerary accordingly. Doing so lets you maximize your time in the city while minimizing your exposure to crowded areas and lengthy lineups.

Buy tickets in advance: Many popular attractions offer the option to buy tickets online, saving you time waiting in long lines. For example, you can buy tickets to the Louvre Museum online and skip the line when you arrive.

Visit during off-peak hours: A good strategy for avoiding crowds at tourist hotspots is to go there early or late. For example, the Eiffel Tower is usually less crowded in the morning or at night, and you'll have a better chance of enjoying the sights without feeling overwhelmed.

Take breaks: Don't try to see everything in one day. Take breaks throughout the day to rest and recharge. Find a quiet spot in a park or a cafe and take a break from the crowds.

Choose less popular attractions: Many attractions in Paris are just as interesting as the popular ones but less crowded. For example, you can visit the Musée d'Orsay instead of the Louvre Museum or the Parc des Buttes-Chaumont instead of the Jardin des Tuileries.

Paris has many hidden gems that are less crowded than the popular tourist areas. Consider exploring neighbourhoods like Montmartre or the Marais district, where you can find quaint streets and local shops.

Get away from the city: If you need a break from the crowds, consider taking a day trip to a nearby town or village. Many charming towns, such as Versailles, Fontainebleau, and Giverny, are within easy reach of Paris.

Use noise-cancelling headphones: If the noise of the crowds is overwhelming, consider using noise-cancelling headphones. This can help block out the noise and create a more peaceful environment.

Do what you need to ensure your health and happiness. Don't be afraid to take breaks, switch up your itinerary, or seek out quieter areas when you need a break from the crowds.

RECOMMENDATIONS FOR LESSER-KNOWN ATTRACTIONS THAT ARE WORTH A VISIT

Paris has many lesser-known attractions that are worth a visit. Instead of sticking to the main tourist areas, visit some of Paris's lesser-known neighbourhoods. These areas are home to many locals and offer a more authentic Parisian experience.

Here are some recommendations:

Musée Rodin: Housed in a stunning mansion with gardens in the 7th arrondissement, this museum showcases the works of the French sculptor Auguste Rodin.

Canal Saint-Martin: The inhabitants and tourists visit this picturesque waterway in the 10th arrondissement. Take a boat ride, picnic by the water, or shop until you drop at the local boutiques and cafes.

Sainte-Chapelle: This stunning Gothic chapel is on the Île de la Cité and features beautiful stained glass windows.

This little Gothic church is more stunning than the nearby Notre Dame Cathedral. The interior decoration is excellent, and it is (mainly) original. It has some of the last original stained glass windows in France. In a word, it's stunning. Those with museum passes can avoid the lengthy wait. The price of admission is 11.00 Euros.

Musée de la Chasse et de la Nature: This museum in the Marais neighbourhood is dedicated to hunting and nature and features art and artefacts related to these themes.

Parc des Buttes-Chaumont: This park in the 19th arrondissement is one of the largest in Paris and features a beautiful lake, a waterfall, and a suspension bridge.

La Promenade Plantée: This elevated park in the 12th arrondissement is built on an old railway viaduct and features gardens, sculptures, and great city views.

Père Lachaise Cemetery: Many well-known persons, like Oscar Wilde, Jim Morrison, and Edith Piaf, are buried in this old cemetery in the 20th arrondissement.

The Pere-Lachaise Cemetery is the French capital's most well-known burial ground. It's the most frequented cemetery in the world, and with good reason; it's serene and eerily beautiful. Though it was established in 1804 as a burial ground, locals found it unacceptable due to its distance from the town centre.

Because of this, just 13 graves in Père Lachaise were in their first year. But, authorities devised a plan to move the bodies of two of Paris's most famous artists, Molière and Jean de La Fontaine, to Père Lachaise. Everyone after that wished to be laid to rest in this cemetery.

Musée de l'Orangerie: This museum in the Tuileries Gardens features works by impressionist and post-impressionist artists, including Monet's famous Water Lilies paintings.

These are a few of the many lesser-known sights to see in Paris.

CHAPTER 4: EATING AND DRINKING LIKE A LOCAL

Among the world's best cities for food and drink, Paris is often ranked high. The Michelin-starred restaurants that line the streets of Paris serve authentic French cuisines such as coq au vin, escargots, and bouillabaisse.

The dining scene in Paris is excellent, and French cuisine is well-known worldwide. You must try the cheese, pastries, and bread if you're in France. Wine, Champagne, and cocktails are widely available at many pubs and cafes in the city.

French food has a rich cultural heritage deeply rooted in its history. Among the many delicious delicacies in the country are freshly baked bread (especially baguettes), outstanding local cheeses, and plentiful wine. Hot ham and cheese sandwiches (croque monsieurs), beef stew (pot au feu), steak and fries (steak frites), and if you're feeling adventurous, frog legs (or escargot, or snails, or live goose liver) are all dishes you must have when in France (a fattened duck or goose liver).

Visiting the farmers market, stocking up on food, and having a picnic in one of the city's many parks is a terrific ways to save money.

You may have a good time and save money (around 6-9 EUR per person) at a do-it-yourself restaurant.

It's easy to experience the local cuisine and drink culture in Paris. Expenses for eating out in the city can quickly add up. However, there are still many excellent restaurants that won't break the bank. Some suggestions are as follows:

Bistros and brasseries: Bistros and brasseries are casual, traditional French restaurants that serve classic dishes like steak frites, croque-monsieur, and onion soup. They often offer affordable prix-fixe menus for lunch and dinner.

Crêperies: Crêperies are small, cosy restaurants specialising in crêpes, both sweet and savoury. They are a great option for a light meal or snack.

Ethnic cuisine: Paris has a diverse population, so many affordable restaurants serve delicious ethnic cuisine. For example, you can find excellent Vietnamese food in the 13th and affordable Lebanese food in the 10th arrondissement.

Visit local markets: Paris has many open-air markets for fresh produce, cheeses, bread, and other local products. The Marché d'Aligre in the 12th arrondissement is one of the city's oldest and most popular markets.

Try street food: Paris has a thriving street food scene, with vendors selling everything from crepes and falafel to gourmet hot dogs and Korean fried chicken. Popular street food areas include Rue des Rosiers in the Marais and Rue Montorgueil in the 2nd arrondissement.

Have a picnic: Paris has many beautiful parks and gardens where you can have a picnic with local foods like baguettes, cheese, and wine. Some popular picnic spots include the Champ de Mars near the Eiffel Tower and the Luxembourg Gardens.

Visit wine bars: Wine is an integral part of French culture. Paris has many wine bars where you can try local wines and small plates of food. Some popular wine bars include Le Baron Rouge in the 12th arrondissement and Le Verre Volé in the 10th arrondissement.

Visit local patisseries: Paris is famous for its pastries and desserts, and there are many local patisseries where you can try macarons, croissants, and other sweet treats. Some popular patisseries include Ladurée in the Champs-Elysées and Pierre Hermé in the Marais.

Cafes: Paris is also famous for its cafes, which serve coffee, tea, and light snacks such as croissants and pain au chocolat. Many cafes have outdoor seating, making them great places for people-watching.

These are just a few options for experiencing Parisian cuisine and drinking as a true local. The city's culinary scene constantly evolves, so there's always something new to discover.

TIPS FOR ORDERING FOOD IN FRENCH AND NAVIGATING MENUS

French is the official language in Paris, but most people in the tourist industry speak English. It's always helpful to learn a few basic French phrases, though, as it shows respect for the local culture.

Communicating with locals and navigating menus can be challenging if you don't speak French, but there are ways to overcome language barriers in Paris.

Here are some tips for ordering food in French and navigating menus:

Learn basic French phrases: Even if you don't speak French fluently, learning basic phrases can be helpful when ordering food. For example, "Bonjour" means hello, "S'il vous plaît" means please, and "Merci" means thank you.

Study menu terms: Familiarize yourself with common menu terms in French, such as "entrée" for an appetizer, "plat principal" for the main course, and "dessert" for dessert. Additionally, you can check out translation resources for dishes you're interested in trying.

Ask for recommendations: If you're unsure what to order or are unfamiliar with some menu items, don't be afraid to ask the server for recommendations or explanations.

Be clear about dietary restrictions: If you have any dietary restrictions or allergies, communicate this clearly to the server. You can say "Je suis allergique à [insert allergy]" or "Je suis végétarien(ne)" for vegetarian.

Don't rush: In France, dining is meant to be a leisurely experience. Take your time perusing the menu, and don't feel rushed to order immediately.

Use a translation app: If you're still unsure about certain menu items or phrases, you can use a translation app on your phone to help you.

Look for English menus: Many restaurants in tourist areas have menus in both French and English, so look for places that offer English menus.

Point to items: If you're having trouble communicating, try pointing to items on the menu or using gestures to indicate what you want. This can be an effective way to order food or drinks without speaking the language.

Remember, it's okay if you're not fluent in French. Most Parisians speak some English, and many restaurants in tourist areas have English translations on their menus. Try to communicate in French and be respectful, and you should have no problem ordering delicious food in Paris.

CHAPTER 5: FINDING BUDGET-FRIENDLY ACCOMMODATION

Finding affordable and suitable accommodation in Paris can be challenging, but there are ways to make the process easier.

Before looking for accommodation, determine your budget. This will help you narrow your options and avoid wasting time looking at places out of your price range.

Paris offers a variety of accommodation options, including hotels, hostels, apartments, and vacation rentals. Consider what type of accommodation would best suit your needs and budget.

Paris has many hotels, hostels, and Airbnb options. The best areas to stay are near the Eiffel Tower, the Champs-Élysées, or the Marais district.

Paris hotels are notoriously pricey and have many options, so finding a place to stay might easily cost you a month's pay.

Finding budget-friendly accommodation in Paris can be challenging, but I have some suggestions that could be useful:

Consider staying in a hostel: Hostels are a great option for budget travellers as they offer dormitory-style rooms at a much lower cost than hotels. Many hostels also have private rooms available if you prefer more privacy.

Book in advance: Booking your accommodation in advance can often save you money, especially when travelling during peak tourist season. Look for deals online and compare prices across different booking platforms.

Stay in a less touristy area: Accommodation prices tend to be higher in popular tourist areas such as the Champs-Élysées and Montmartre. Consider staying in a less touristy area like the 11th or 12th arrondissements, which still offer plenty of amenities and easy access to public transportation.

Look for apartment rentals: Renting an apartment can be a good option if you're travelling with a group or planning to stay in Paris for an extended period. Websites like Airbnb and VRBO offer various options at different price points.

Consider a homestay: One of the best ways to experience Parisian culture on a budget is to stay with a local host. Websites like Homestay and Couchsurfing can help you find hosts in Paris.

Stay outside of the city centre: Accommodation prices tend to be lower outside of the city centre, so consider staying in a suburb or nearby town and taking public transportation into Paris. This can also offer a different perspective on the city and allow you to explore more off-the-beaten-path areas.

Consider sharing with others: If you're travelling with friends or family, consider sharing an apartment or vacation rental. This can be a cost-effective way to enjoy more spacious and comfortable accommodations.

Using these tips, you can find affordable and suitable accommodation in Paris that meets your budget and preferences. Review reviews and research before booking any accommodation to ensure it meets your budget and preferences.

OVERVIEW OF PARIS' DIFFERENT NEIGHBORHOODS AND ACCOMMODATION OPTIONS

Paris is divided into different neighbourhoods, each with its character and attractions. Research the neighbourhoods you are interested in and choose one that is convenient and safe for you.

There are 20 arrondissements in Paris, each with its special charm and personality. Here's a quick rundown of a few of the city's most fashionable areas and some examples of the lodging options you might expect to find there.

Le Marais: This historic district is known for its winding streets, trendy boutiques, and lively nightlife. Accommodation options include trendy boutique hotels, stylish apartments, and charming bed and breakfasts.

Montmartre: Located on a hill overlooking the city, Montmartre is home to the famous Sacré-Cœur Basilica and is known for its bohemian vibe. Accommodation options include cosy guesthouses, small hotels, and affordable hostels.

Saint-Germain-des-Prés: This upscale neighbourhood is known for its art galleries, high-end shopping, and chic cafes. Accommodation options include luxury hotels, stylish apartments, and charming bed and breakfasts.

The Latin Quarter: This historic neighbourhood is home to Sorbonne University and is known for its lively atmosphere and intellectual vibe. Accommodation options include budget-friendly hostels, affordable hotels, and cosy guesthouses.

The Champs-Élysées: This famous avenue has high-end shops and luxury hotels. Accommodation options include luxurious five-star hotels, chic boutique hotels, and stylish apartments.

The Eiffel Tower and Trocadéro: Besides being home to some of the city's most opulent hotels, this neighbourhood is famous for its breathtaking views of the Eiffel Tower. Accommodation options include opulent five-star hotels, stylish apartments, and cosy breakfasts.

The Bastille: This former working-class neighbourhood is now a trendy hotspot known for its nightlife and music scene. Accommodation options include affordable hostels, cosy guesthouses, and stylish apartments.

Canal Saint-Martin: This trendy neighbourhood is home to hip cafes, trendy boutiques, and beautiful parks. Accommodation options include stylish boutique hotels, charming bed and breakfasts, and cosy apartments.

No matter what neighbourhood you choose, you can expect to find various accommodation options to suit all budgets and preferences.

RECOMMENDATIONS FOR AFFORDABLE HOTELS AND HOSTELS

Some suggestions for cheap accommodations in Paris are provided below.

Inn of the Rock: Hotel Rochechouart is the epitome of classic elegance; it is easy to imagine Hemingway dining here. The upper level features spacious apartments in place of the usual cramped "maid's quarters" (chambres de bonne). The bar's elevated location provides unparalleled views of the Sacré-Coeur.

At the Hotel Notre-Dame des Arts: The Hôtel Dame des Arts is the best hotel in Paris. Like other stunning roofs recently built, this one comes close to touching Notre Dame's iconic towers. Thanks to the hotel's sophisticated decor, on-site sauna and gym, and signature scent, you'll feel like you've stepped into a scene from a French love film. The Saint-Michel subway station is easily accessible through a short walk.

You'll find the stylish Generator Paris hostel in the 10th arrondissement, close to the Canal Saint-Martin. It has private rooms, dormitory-style beds, a restaurant, a bar, and regular gatherings for its guests.

Les Piaules is a low-cost option for lodging in the hip Belleville area, featuring private and shared rooms, a rooftop patio, and a bar.

The Eiffel Tower is conveniently placed near the Hotel Eiffel Turenne, a low-cost accommodation in the 7th arrondissement. There is a daily breakfast buffet and cosy accommodations available.

Hotel Pun: You may find this unusual lodging option in the 9th arrondissement, not far from the hipster enclave of Pigalle. It has a bar, a daily breakfast buffet, and colourful rooms.

Hotel Excelsior Latin is a cheap option in the Latin Quarter, close to many of the city's best sights. There is a daily breakfast buffet and cosy accommodations available.

The trendy Loft Boutique Hostel & Hotel is in the 20th arrondissement, near the beautiful Pere Lachaise Cemetery. Dorms and private rooms and a bar and rooftop lounge are available.

St. Christopher's Inn Gare du Nord is a famous hostel because of its proximity to the Gare du Nord railway station. It has both individual and shared rooms, as well as a restaurant and bar.

The Hotel Duc De Saint Simon in the 6eme epitomizes the charming French petit hotel, with all the pretty chintz you could want.

The Hôtel Bulgari de Paris is a more stylish option for people who prefer Italian to French room service than its enormous neighbours because it resembles a contemporary apartment complex. You'll find one of the best fitness centres in town at this hotel, complete with a swimming pool and a hot tub.

At the Hôtel Elysée, you may relax in one of the spacious suites, each of which features a marble bathroom outfitted in the style of the eponymous residences in Paris. You won't believe how near you are to the action of the Champs-Élysées when you stay in one of the quiet rooms on the top floor.

The lovely and opulent Hotel Raphael is placed on Avenue Kléber in the 16th arrondissement. The interiors are elegantly designed to befit a Parisian establishment, blending styles from the Louis XVI and Belle Epoque eras.

During the fall of 2021, the Louvre Post Office was remodelled into a hotel called Madame Rêve. Early risers who attend yoga on the rooftop can glimpse the Eiffel Tower and the metropolis below.

Despite the high ceilings and elaborate chandeliers, the space below the restaurant and cocktail bar is warm and inviting thanks to the soothing colour palette of goldenrod yellow, burgundy, and wood. Thanks to the hotel's location, day visits to both the Louvre and the Marais are quick and easy. The Stohrer Patisserie is a short stroll away, and it's a great place to get some pastries to go with your morning coffee.

It's hard to dispute that The Ritz-Paris is the most illustrious hotel in the world. Afternoon tea at Salon Proust and a drink at the world-famous Bar Hemingway are musts on any trip to Paris. The two establishments will whisk you to a more luxurious era with Louis XV-style furnishings, rare volumes, canopied beds, and gilded chandeliers.

You'll feel right at home in the cosy rooms of the Hôtel du Sentier, nestled on a quiet street in Paris's 2nd arrondissement. The basic yet chic design keeps all the spaces bright and airy, and views of the cityscape in all their glory are an added treat. The convenient location of the café on the ground floor makes it possible to obtain an oat milk latte or a bottle of Sancerre at any time of the day.

There are plenty of cheaper hotels and hostels in the city than the ones listed here. The greatest choice that fits your needs and your wallet can be found by reading reviews and comparing pricing.

TIPS FOR FINDING ALTERNATIVE ACCOMMODATION

Here are some tips for finding alternative accommodation options like Airbnbs and house swaps in Paris:

Check multiple websites: While Airbnb is the most well-known alternative accommodation platform, many other websites offer similar options. Some popular sites to check to include Vrbo, HomeAway, FlipKey, and Booking.com.

Look for neighbourhoods outside the tourist centre: Staying in a less central neighbourhood can often be more affordable and provide a more authentic experience. Look for neighbourhoods like Belleville, Montmartre, or the 11th and 12th arrondissements.

Consider a house swap: One of the best ways to save money on lodging and get a taste of local culture is to swap houses with a local. Many websites facilitate house swaps, such as HomeExchange and Love Home Swap.

Check for discounts and promotions: Many platforms offer discounts or promotions for first-time users or longer stays. Be sure to check for these before booking.

Read reviews carefully: Before booking, be sure to read reviews carefully to get a sense of the experience others have had with the host or property.

Communicate with the host: Once you've found a property you're interested in, communicate with the host to ask any questions and ensure that the property meets your needs.

Be aware of local regulations: Paris has strict regulations on short-term rentals, so be sure to check the legality of the property before booking. Some hosts may require you to sign a rental agreement and provide a copy of your passport or ID.

CHAPTER 6: STAYING SAFE AND AVOIDING SCAMS

Paris is generally safe, but it's important to stay aware of your surroundings and monitor your belongings like in any big city. Be cautious in touristy areas where pickpocketing is common.

It's understandable to have safety concerns when travelling alone or at night in any city, including Paris. However, you can minimize potential risks with precautions and common sense.

Here are some tips for staying safe and avoiding scams while travelling in Paris:

Be aware of your surroundings: Keep your senses on high alert, especially when visiting popular tourist destinations. Watch for pickpockets, and be cautious of people trying to distract you.

Use common sense: Use common sense and follow your instincts. If something feels off, trust your gut and take precautions.

Avoid walking alone at night: Never wander late if you can help, especially if the neighbourhood is poorly lit or abandoned. Take a taxi or public transportation instead.

Keep your valuables secure: Keep your valuables, such as your passport, wallet, and phone, always secure. Consider using a money belt or cross-body bag to keep your belongings safe.

Be cautious of scams: Be wary of people offering unsolicited help or trying to sell you something on the street. Common scams in Paris include the gold ring scam and the petition scam.

Use official transportation: Stick to official taxi stands or ride-sharing apps like Uber or Lyft. Avoid using unlicensed taxis or getting into cars with strangers.

Stay in well-lit and secure areas: Choose accommodations in well-lit and secure areas. Check reviews and ratings before booking to ensure the property is safe and secure.

Learn basic French phrases: Some can help you communicate with locals and navigate the city more easily. It can also help you avoid misunderstandings and potential scams.

Don't trust strangers: Be cautious of strangers approaching you, particularly at night. Be wary of anyone who offers you unsolicited help or asks for money.

Dial 112 for help in an immediate need.

My number one piece of guidance is to make sure you have adequate travel insurance. A travel insurance policy will cover you in the event of an accident, illness, theft, or trip cancellation, and all bases are covered in case of an emergency. Because I've needed it so much in the past, it's now an essential item for any trip I take.

OVERVIEW OF COMMON SCAMS AND SAFETY CONCERNS IN PARIS

Visitors to Paris can feel secure in the city's relatively low crime rate, but like any major city, there are some safety concerns and scams to be aware of. Violence against tourists is extremely rare in Paris. Yet, as with most large urban centres, pickpocketing and other forms of petty theft are possible, especially on overcrowded public transportation and popular tourist destinations. To avoid having your goods stolen or lost, you should never display or leave them where they may be easily accessed.

Some people will trick you into signing a petition in exchange for money. Respectfully decline the offer of anyone asking you to join a petition, and you will be safe from further pressure.

Here are common scams and safety concerns in Paris:

Pickpocketing: Pickpocketing is a common problem in crowded tourist areas and on public transportation. It would help if you always were mindful of your whereabouts and the whereabouts of your valuables.

Street scams: Street scams are also common in Paris. The gold ring scam involves someone asking if you dropped a gold ring and then offering to sell it at a discount. The petition scam involves people approaching you with a clipboard and asking for your signature or a donation.

ATM skimming: ATM skimming is a growing problem in Paris. Be sure to use ATMs in well-lit and public areas, and cover the keypad when entering your PIN.

Traffic accidents: Traffic can be heavy and chaotic in Paris, so be cautious when crossing the street and be aware of traffic patterns.

Terrorist attacks: There have been multiple terrorist strikes in Paris recently. While the likelihood of an attack is still low, it's important to be aware of your surroundings and follow the guidance of local authorities.

Stay safe in Paris, know your surroundings, keep your valuables close, and use common sense. If someone on the street approaches you, be cautious and keep your distance. If you feel uncomfortable or threatened, seek help from local authorities or other people around you.

TIPS FOR STAYING SAFE WHILE TRAVELING ALONE OR AT NIGHT

Women travelling alone can feel comfortable in this area; however, the usual warnings apply (never walk home alone late at night if you've been drinking).

Avoid going out late at night in areas like Gare du Nord, Stalingrad, Jaures, and Les Halles if you want to play it safe.

Travelling alone or at night can present additional safety concerns. Here are some tips for staying safe:

Stick to well-lit and busy areas: When travelling at night, stick to well-lit areas with plenty of foot traffic. Avoid dark or deserted streets, and stay alert to your surroundings.

Plan your route: If you're travelling alone, plan your route and let someone know where you're going and when you expect to arrive.

Avoid displaying valuables: Avoid displaying valuables like jewellery, cameras, and smartphones, especially when travelling alone or at night. Keep your valuables hidden or in a secure bag.

Use transportation services safely: If you're using taxis or ride-sharing services, make sure you're using a reputable service and that the vehicle matches the description provided. Avoid getting into unmarked or unlicensed vehicles.

Trust your instincts: Don't ignore your gut feelings of danger if you ever sense them. Leave the area as quickly and safely as possible. If necessary, seek help from local authorities or other people around you.

Research your accommodation: If you're travelling alone, research your accommodation in advance to ensure it's in a safe area and has adequate security measures.

Maintain relationships with your family and friends: If you must travel alone, stay with loved ones back home and tell them where you are and how you're doing.

Following these tips can help ensure your safety while travelling alone or at night.

RECOMMENDATIONS FOR NEIGHBOURHOODS AND AREAS TO AVOID

While there is no reason to be overly concerned about your safety in Paris, there are several neighbourhoods you should avoid or approach with caution, especially late at night. Places with greater crime rates or a lower reputation for safety include:

Châtelet-Les Halles is infamous for its high pickpocketing rates and other theft forms due to its dense population and overpowering nightlife.

Even though Barbès is well-known for its many cultural offers and bustling street markets, the region might feel hazardous at night due to its high population density and low security.

The Gare du Nord is a busy transportation centre, but it may also be a target for pickpockets and other con artists.

Pigalle: Although famous for its nightlife and adult entertainment, this district is also infamous for its seediness and danger after dark.

Stalingrad: The neighbourhood is notorious for its high concentration of drug users and other criminals, making it frightening at night.

To be clear, these places are not inherently unsafe, and many people visit them without incident. However, one should always be alert, especially at night, and take precautions to protect oneself and one's property.

CHAPTER 7: SHOPPING LIKE A LOCAL

The shopping scene in Paris directly reflects the city's status as one of the world's fashion capitals. There is something for every kind of shopper to do in Paris, from high-end luxury stores to street-side flea markets and everything in between.

The most famous shopping street in Paris is the Avenue des Champs-Élysées, where you'll find a mix of high-end designer stores like Louis Vuitton, Gucci, and Cartier and more affordable shops like Zara and H&M.

Another popular shopping destination is the Rue Saint-Honoré, home to the flagship stores of many luxury fashion brands like Chanel, Hermès, and Saint Laurent.

Plenty of smaller neighbourhoods and streets exist for those looking for more unique and off-the-beaten-path shopping experiences. The Marais neighbourhood is a favourite among locals and visitors alike, with its narrow streets lined with independent boutiques, vintage shops, and trendy cafes. The Canal Saint-Martin area is also popular for its artisanal stores and independent fashion boutiques.

The markets of Paris are another reason the city is so well-known; these markets sell everything from antiques to vintage goods and fresh fruit. The Marché aux Puces de Saint-Ouen is one of the largest flea markets in the world and is widely regarded as the most well-known market in the city. It is known for its extensive collection of vintage and antique items.

Paris is a great place to go shopping because it has plenty to offer everyone, whether you're seeking high-end luxury apparel or a more bohemian shopping experience. Just make sure you're prepared to deal with the crowds and the occasional case of sticker shock because many of the city's most popular shopping sites tend to charge somewhat high prices.

RECOMMENDATIONS FOR LOCAL BOUTIQUES, MARKETS, AND THRIFT SHOPS

It can be difficult to find decent places to shop in Paris that are not tourist traps, but it is not impossible.

You can find one-of-a-kind, genuine items sold by locals in many of Paris's small markets, such as the Marché d'Aligre and the Marché des Enfants Rouges. Souvenirs, fresh food, and other products can all be found at these non-touristy markets.

There are numerous local boutiques in Paris where you can buy one-of-a-kind garments, accessories, and furnishings. Try to find locally owned establishments in less visited sections of town.

The Champs-Élysées may be the most well-known shopping boulevard in Paris, but it also has a reputation for being overpriced and crowded with tourists. Try your luck in the city's back alleys and less touristy neighbourhoods for more interesting finds and better prices.

There are many thrift stores and vintage boutiques in Paris where you can find one-of-a-kind products at reasonable prices. You can find fantastic discounts at the flea markets in the Saint-Ouen neighbourhood or the antique shops in the nearby Marais district.

Try to find shops that specialize in selling regional specialities. You can support local businesses and find one-of-a-kind treasures at the same time by shopping at these stores.

Many places to shop in Paris are not in the typical tourist districts.

If you're looking for truly special and original purchasing opportunities, consider the following suggestions:

Le Marais is a historic district loved by Parisians for its one-of-a-kind boutiques, thrift stores, and art galleries.

This hipster enclave along the banks of the Canal Saint-Martin is famous for its many unique shops selling anything from clothing and accessories to home decor and art.

The 9th arrondissement's picturesque Rue des Martyrs is a mecca for gourmets, thanks to its abundance of artisanal bakeries, cheese shops, and wine merchants.

In the 2nd arrondissement, you'll find the lively pedestrian street, Rue Montorgueil, lined with stores selling everything from fresh fruit to handmade cheeses.

The Saint-Ouen Flea Market is one of the largest in the world and is located on the outskirts of Paris. It is a great place to find antiques, collectables, and unique apparel from bygone eras.

Merci is a popular concept store in the Marais district of Paris, known for its well-edited assortment of clothing, home decor, literature, and relaxed shopping environment.

Le Bon Marché is a historic Parisian department store that sells high-end clothing, accessories, and even antiques. Those interested in beautiful art nouveau design should pay a visit.

The 12th arrondissement is home to the open-air market Marché d'Aligre, where you may find a wide variety of goods, including food (including fresh produce), drink (including cheese and wine), and antiques (including apparel).

When you purchase at Kg Shop, you'll get a one-of-a-kind vintage shopping experience because everything is priced by kilo instead of each item. In this shop, you can find unique vintage items at reasonable prices.

Free'P'Star - This thrift shop has multiple locations throughout the city and is known for its affordable prices and eclectic selection of vintage and secondhand clothing.

Galeries Lafayette - This department store is known for its stunning Art Deco architecture and high-end fashion offerings. Even if you're not in the market for luxury goods, it's worth a visit to admire the beauty of the building.

Rélique: Visit Rélique, located near République, for deliciously quirky antique shopping.

Maison Dior: Housed within the newly opened Dior flagship store on Montaigne Avenue, Maison Dior is a carefully curated extension of the historical brand. The eating area is decorated in a colour scheme of red, black, and white from the brand's past collections. In addition to the mismatched houndstooth seats, Maison Dior furnishes each table with fine tableware.

Antoinette de Poisson: Visitors interested in history, aesthetics, and paper should visit Antoinette de Poisson. The shop, together with its secret courtyard, is a tranquil haven where the passage of time seems to have stopped. The company still uses traditional methods to produce domino papers with intricate designs like flowers and geometric shapes. This sheet protected books and small boxes throughout the 18th century. The same may be said about the historical romance-infused perfume, wallpaper, and home accessories sold by Antoinette de Poisson.

Dary's is the most paradisiacal antique jewellery boutique ever, stocked with works of art from the great houses and the unknown.

Michele Aragon and Simrane: If you're looking for a kilim-covered armchair in the 6th, look no further than Michele Aragon, a veritable Aladdin's cave of unique and beautiful homewares. Simrane, located just across the corner from Michele Aragon, is France's first and only Indian block print exporter and carries every paisley tablecloth pattern imaginable.

Ms Pascale Monvoisin: Pascale's jewellery is beautiful, and her shop on Rue Mont Thabor in Paris is the best place to buy it. Whether it's the shells, the tiny gold bits, or the vibrant hues, nearly every piece of her jewellery transports me to a tropical paradise.

Nuovo: Nuovo is the best shopping centre. It's a modest vintage shop packed with trendy items for women. The proprietor selects items not based on labelling but on personal preference.

Rouje: If you're looking for the latest in French girl fashion, you must look no further than Rouje, Jeanne Damas's flagship boutique.

There are many more places to shop in Paris. The key to finding the best local boutiques, markets, and thrift shops is to explore the city's different neighbourhoods and watch for unique, independent stores.

When shopping like a local in Paris, remember that many independent stores and boutiques close on Sundays and Mondays, so plan your shopping accordingly.

Additionally, don't be afraid to explore smaller side streets and alleys, as some of the best shopping experiences in Paris can be found off the beaten path.

TIPS FOR BARGAINING AND FINDING DEALS

Bargaining is not typically practised in Paris, especially in established stores and markets. However, you can still find deals and discounts by:

Shopping during sale seasons: Sales are strictly regulated in Paris, but you can find great discounts during the official sales periods in January and July and mid-season sales in March and September.

Visiting flea markets and thrift shops: You can find unique and affordable items at flea markets like the famous Marché aux Puces de Saint-Ouen and thrift shops like Guerrisol and Emmaüs.

Exploring local markets: At reasonable prices, markets like Marché d'Aligre and Marché des Enfants Rouges offer fresh produce, cheese, and other food items.

Avoid touristy areas: Shopping in popular tourist areas like Champs-Élysées can be expensive, so exploring smaller neighbourhoods and local markets for affordable finds is best.

Checking out concept stores: Paris has many concept stores that sell unique items from local designers and artisans, which can be affordable and of high quality.

Always compare prices before purchasing, and keep your belongings safe while shopping in crowded areas.

CHAPTER 8: EMBRACING THE CITY'S ART AND CULTURE

Paris has a rich artistic and cultural heritage; also, guests can choose from many attractions. Paris is famous for its art and culture, and there are many ways to embrace it during your visit. Here are some tips:

Visit museums and galleries: Paris is home to many world-renowned museums, such as the Louvre, Musée d'Orsay, and Centre Pompidou, as well as smaller galleries that feature emerging and established artists.

These museums house incredible collections of art and artefacts from around the world.

Numerous galleries throughout Paris showcase works from established and emerging artists. The Marais and Saint-Germain-des-Prés neighbourhoods are particularly known for their galleries.

Historic monuments: Paris is home to many historic monuments, including the Eiffel Tower, Notre Dame Cathedral, and the Arc de Triomphe. These landmarks are not only impressive to look at but also offer insight into the city's history.

Attend cultural events and performances: Paris is known for its rich cultural offerings, including theatre, opera, ballet, and music performances. Check listings for current events during your visit.

Theatre, opera, and ballet: The Opéra Garnier and the Théâtre des Champs-Élysées are only two of the world-famous theatres that can be found in Paris. The city is also known for its ballet companies, such as the Paris Opera Ballet.

Explore street art: Paris has many impressive murals and installations, especially in neighbourhoods like Belleville, the 13th arrondissement, and Montmartre.

Wander through historic neighbourhoods: Paris has many historic neighbourhoods, such as Le Marais, Latin Quarter, and Montmartre, where you can explore narrow streets, ancient architecture, and local shops and cafes.

Attend festivals and cultural celebrations: Paris has many festivals and cultural celebrations throughout the year, such as the Fête de la Musique, Paris Plages, and the Paris Fashion Week.

Remember to keep an open mind and respect local customs and traditions while embracing Parisian art and culture.

There's no need to leave Paris without experiencing the music that drew some of the world's greatest musicians and artists there in the first place, whether your preference is for cutting-edge clubs or traditional jazz haunts. The city is famous for its plethora of excellent jazz clubs, and it opened in 1984, yet Le Duc des Lombards has already established itself as one of the city's premier jazz venues. It's not just the drinks at Harry's Bar that are amazing; the tunes are, too.

RECOMMENDATIONS FOR MUSEUMS, GALLERIES, AND THEATRES

Paris is home to numerous world-class museums, galleries, and theatres. Here are some recommendations:

Louvre Museum: One of the world's largest and most visited museums, the Louvre is home to an extensive collection of art and artefacts, including the famous Mona Lisa painting.

While the Louvre is well worth seeing, visiting the adjacent Musée des Arts Décoratifs is also recommended. Featuring a stunning collection of vintage and contemporary furnishings (including Louis XVI chairs and Charlotte Perriand shelves) and a regularly rotating showcase of the season's most noteworthy garments. In preparation for the 2024 Olympic Games, a sportswear look is in the works.

Musée d'Orsay: Impressionist and post-impressionist masterpieces, such as those by Monet, Van Gogh, and Renoir, are on display in this museum, located in a beautifully converted train station.

Centre Pompidou: This museum is known for its bold architecture and modern and contemporary art collection.

Musée Rodin: This museum houses a collection of Auguste Rodin's sculptures and a lovely outdoor sculpture garden.

Palais Garnier: One of the world's most famous opera houses, the Palais Garnier is an architectural masterpiece and a must-visit for music lovers.

Treat yourself to a night of dance at the Palais Garnier, a Parisian monument that is both famous and well-deserved for its sumptuous, Napoleonic-style architecture.

Théâtre du Châtelet: This legendary theatre has hosted various performances over the years, including but not limited to opera, ballet, and musicals.

Fondation Louis Vuitton: This contemporary art museum, designed by architect Frank Gehry, features a stunning glass and steel building and a rotating modern and contemporary art collection.

Musée de l'Orangerie: Located in the Tuileries Gardens, Monet's Water Lilies are among the many works of impressionist and post-impressionist art displayed in this museum.

La Cinémathèque française: This museum and archive is dedicated to the history of cinema and features a collection of over 40,000 films.

Atelier des Lumières: This immersive digital art centre projects art onto the walls and floors of a former foundry, creating a unique and unforgettable experience.

L'Atelier des Lumières, a new alternative art space, is a must-see (€18, open daily). The artworks on display in the revolving exhibition are brought to life by the accompaniment of music using artificial intelligence, creating a truly immersive experience for visitors of all senses. If you've ever wanted to know what entering a painting is like, here's your chance.

The artists of 59 Rivoli are out to prove that artwork need not cost a million dollars (free entry, donations encouraged, closed on Mondays). The six stories once occupied illegally, now feature a dynamic collection of artworks, including murals, sculptures, and political messages. As a result, guests have a good chance of witnessing the artists in residence at work (or chatting over coffee).

Pinault Collection: No trip to Paris should omit a stop at the brand-new Pinault Collection. The structure was once a commodities trading centre known as the bourse de commerce, but now it serves as the dignified and majestic home to a one-of-a-kind collection of artwork by well-known and up-and-coming artists. The enormous dome housing the current Urs Fischer exhibition left me speechless. If you want to shop after your visit, the Pinault is conveniently located on rue Saint Honoré.

Musée de la Chasse et de la Nature: The Musée de la Chasse et de la Nature, a museum dedicated to hunting and the natural world hidden away in a breathtakingly magnificent hôtel particulier in the heart of Le Marais, is one of the city's many hidden gems. A highlight is the museum's deliciously gruesome taxidermy displays. Still, the museum avoids being too fusty by commissioning modern artists like Sterling Ruby and Jeff Koons to create pieces in dialogue with its holdings. Every time you visit, you'll discover something new.

These are just a few of Paris's many art and cultural offerings, and there is something for everyone, from classical to contemporary, from high-brow to pop culture.

TIPS FOR ATTENDING EVENTS AND FESTIVALS

Paris is home to many cultural events, such as concerts, exhibitions, and festivals, that offer a chance to experience local art and entertainment. Check out local newspapers or website listings to find events that interest you.

Each year on July 14th, Paris hosts several magnificent activities commemorating the infamous storming of the Bastille during the French Revolution. The medieval Bastille stronghold in Paris stood as a symbol of royal power, and in capturing it, the Revolution achieved a major victory.

Nowadays, people go to Champ de Mars, or the Jardins du Trocadéro, for the best views of the endless fireworks display and massive procession broadcast live worldwide.

Paris hosts a massive outdoor film festival throughout July and August in the 9th arrondissement's Park de la Villette, complete with an inflatable screen. It's quite well-liked by neighbourhood residents, many of whom bring picnics and bottles of wine. Moreover, there is no cost associated with participating.

Paris is known for its fashion and style, and Paris Fashion Week is a major event in the fashion industry. It takes place twice a year, in January and September, and showcases the latest collections from top designers. If you're interested in attending fashion week, planning and securing tickets or invitations in advance is important.

Bastille Day, or la Fête Nationale, is France's national holiday, celebrated on July 14th. In honour of the founding of the new French country, this monument was built to remember the day the Bastille prison was stormed during the French Revolution. Festival-goers can enjoy parades, fireworks, and live performances to celebrate the holiday. One of the best places to celebrate Bastille Day in Paris is on the Champs-Élysées, with a military parade and a spectacular fireworks display. It's also a popular day for picnics in the city's parks and gardens.

Paris is a city that offers numerous events and festivals throughout the year. Here are some tips for attending them:

Check the schedule in advance: Many events and festivals have a schedule, so check it beforehand to avoid missing out on something you want to see.

Buy tickets early: If an event or festival requires tickets, buy them early to avoid disappointment or long lines. You can often purchase tickets online.

Arrive early: Some events and festivals can get very crowded, so arriving early can help you get a good spot and avoid long lines.

Be prepared for the weather: Paris weather can be unpredictable, so check the forecast and bring appropriate clothing or gear for outdoor events.

Respect local customs: Some events or festivals may have specific customs or traditions, so respecting them is important.

Immerse yourself in the culture: Attending events and festivals is a great way to learn about local culture and traditions, so embrace the experience and try to engage with locals or other attendees to learn more.

CHAPTER 9: DAY TRIPS FROM PARIS

Paris is the busiest (and most expensive) in the summer. Even though the weather is wonderful, many people will be out enjoying it, so many will wait in line to see the most popular sights. Remember to plan for lodging and sightseeing if you travel during the summer. The low 20s (high 70s F) are where you can expect the mercury to hover regularly during the summer.

It's best to go in May, early June, late September, or early October. You'll find fewer people and pleasant temperatures during these times. The weather is pleasant, with average highs in the 20s to lows in the mid-to high-70s (68-73 degrees Fahrenheit), making spring and summer great times to take long walks outside without a heavy coat or a hat. You may also expect to pay less for lodging and entertainment during these months.

Even if it's not always warm and sunny in Paris, the city is stunning in the winter. It's also the perfect time to book a hotel or flight at a discount. Though Paris is never without visitors, this time of year is noticeably less busy than others. If you intend to spend much of your time indoors at museums and other historical attractions, this may be an ideal time to visit. This is also the wettest season, and daily highs will be around 44 degrees Fahrenheit (7 degrees Celsius).

My recommended daily budget for a backpacking trip to Paris is 70 Euros. With this money, you can stay in a hostel dormitory, prepare your meals (including picnics), use public transportation, restrict your alcohol consumption, and participate in many free or low-cost activities (such as walking tours and museums).

Your average day in Paris will cost about 150 EUR, covering your private Airbnb room, most of your meals at inexpensive, fast food establishments, a few drinks, the occasional taxi ride, and more expensive activities like visiting the Eiffel Tower the Louvre.

If you have a "luxury" budget of 280 EUR per day or more, you can stay in a cheap hotel, dine out for every meal, take more cabs, drink more, and do more excursions and activities you like.

Nevertheless, this is only the first level of luxury, and any potential outcomes could be possible.

Paris is surrounded by beautiful and historic destinations, making it an excellent base for day trips. Many exciting day trips can be taken from Paris.

Here are some popular day trip options from Paris:

Versailles: Home to the famous Palace of Versailles, this nearby town is a popular destination for visitors to Paris. The palace and gardens are a must-see, and the town has charming shops and restaurants.

Located just outside Paris, the Palace of Versailles is a must-visit attraction for its stunning architecture and beautiful gardens.

A day is needed to see the famous palace from the 17th century. This extravagant palace was originally a hunting lodge that Louis XIV had constructed to remove the nobility from Paris and prevent any possible coups. To serve as a continual reminder to the public that the king possessed ultimate power in the nation, it was expanded and ornamented with countless allegorical images and symbols over the years. If you want to avoid the crowds, visiting the palace on the weekend is your best bet, while the grounds are at their best when the music is playing in the summer. Palace entry is 18 EUR, while complex admission (which includes the gardens) is 27 EUR.

Visit the opulent Palace of Versailles and its vast gardens, just 30 minutes outside Paris by train.

Luxembourg Garden: The Luxembourg Garden, or Jardin du Luxembourg, is a 56-acre public park in the heart of Paris. Over a hundred monuments, statues, and fountains are dotted across the garden's grounds.

Before the French Revolution, the park had been abandoned for years; afterwards, Jean Chalgrin, the Arc de Triomphe designer, began rehabilitating and enlarging the space. Most mornings, this area becomes a bustling training ground for runners. On a sunny day, take your lunch and picnic with the locals in the park.

Giverny: Home to the famous Impressionist painter Claude Monet, Giverny is a beautiful village known for its picturesque landscapes and Monet's house and gardens.

This small town is where Claude Monet lived and painted for many years. Visitors can tour his house and gardens, which served as inspiration for many of his famous works.

Take a trip to the picturesque village of Giverny, where Monet lived and painted many of his famous works. The highlight of the visit is Monet's house and its stunning gardens.

Fontainebleau: This town is home to the beautiful Château de Fontainebleau, which was once the residence of French kings. Visitors can tour the castle, its gardens, and the nearby forest, a popular destination for hikers and rock climbers.

Château de Fontainebleau: This beautiful castle is located about an hour south of Paris and is a UNESCO World Heritage Site. It boasts a stunning collection of artwork and beautiful gardens.

Champagne Region: The Champagne region, located about 2 hours east of Paris, is famous for its sparkling wine and beautiful countryside. Champagne Region: The Champagne region, known for producing the famous sparkling wine, is just a short train ride from Paris. Visitors can tour wineries, taste the local wines, and learn about the history of this beloved beverage.

Plan a day trip to Champagne to tour a winery and sample the region's famous sparkling wine.

Mont Saint-Michel: This stunning island and abbey is located about 4 hours west of Paris and is a UNESCO World Heritage Site.

Visit the stunning island abbey of Mont Saint-Michel, located off the coast of Normandy.

Normandy: The historic region of Normandy, located about 2 hours northwest of Paris, is known for its beautiful beaches, charming towns, and historic sites like the D-Day landing beaches and the Bayeux Tapestry.

Visit the historic D-Day beaches in Normandy and the American Cemetery, paying tribute to the Allied forces that fought in World War II.

Loire Valley: This beautiful region, located about 2 hours south of Paris, is famous for its beautiful chateau and lush countryside.

The Loire Valley is known for its stunning chateaux and beautiful countryside. Visitors can tour the castles, taste wine, and enjoy the region's natural beauty.

Visit the stunning chateaus of the Loire Valley, such as Château de Chambord and Château de Chenonceau, known for their impressive architecture and gardens.

Disneyland Paris: Disneyland Paris is a terrific place to visit with your family or friends if you're searching for enchantment on your vacation.

Reims: Visit the city of Reims, located in the Champagne region, for its beautiful Gothic cathedral and to sample the local Champagne.

These are just a few options, and many more beautiful and historic destinations to explore around Paris. It's best to plan and book transportation and tickets to make the most of your time.

TIPS FOR PLANNING TRANSPORTATION AND ACTIVITIES FOR A DAY TRIP

Here are some tips for planning transportation and activities for a day trip from Paris:

Research transportation options: Look into the options available for your chosen day trip destination. Trains are usually the easiest and fastest way to get to nearby cities and towns, while buses or car rentals may be better for more remote areas. Make sure to book your transportation in advance to avoid any last-minute hassles.

Plan your itinerary: Decide the activities you want to do and the sights you want to see during your day trip. Consider any required admission fees or reservations, and plan your schedule to ensure you have enough time to see everything you want.

Pack appropriately: Check the weather forecast and pack accordingly. Bring comfortable walking shoes, a water bottle, and any necessary medications or items you may need during the day.

Bring a map or guidebook: Even if you plan on using your phone for navigation, it's always a good idea to bring a physical map or guidebook in case your phone dies or you lose service.

Be flexible: Keep in mind that things cannot go as planned, so it's smart to be adaptable and have a backup strategy.

Check return transportation schedules: In advance, check the return transportation schedule and plan accordingly. If you miss the last train or bus, you may need to arrange for alternative transportation or stay overnight.

CHAPTER 10: MAKING THE MOST OF YOUR TIME IN PARIS

Paris is why France is the most visited country in the world. With its world-famous museums, wide boulevards, Belle Epoque architecture, and delicious food, Paris is considered Europe's and the world's cultural epicentre.

Nonetheless, Paris's romanticized reputation plays a role in attracting tourists in addition to the city's actual attractions.

Planning a vacation to Paris might be challenging due to the city's wealth of tourist destinations and activities. Here are some suggestions for making the most of your time in the City of Lights:

Plan: The abundance of attractions necessitates careful preparation. If you're having trouble fitting everything into your day, maybe developing a list of your top priorities would help.

Do some reading up on the area, and list must-sees and experiences. Create a rough schedule to organize your time better.

You may not be able to see every item or monument on your list, so prioritize the ones that are most important to you.

The best cafes and bakeries in Paris don't open until the early morning, so take advantage of this and get a head start on your day. In addition to avoiding crowds, you'll also have more time to look around.

It's best to avoid the crowds at popular museums and attractions by getting there before they open.

There are numerous free things to do in Paris, such as visiting the city's many parks, gardens, and museums. In this way, you may see Paris without breaking the bank.

Take advantage of the city's excellent public transit system to get around Paris quickly and easily. Getting around Paris can get pricey, so investing in a Paris Visite pass or a Navigo card may be worthwhile. If you plan on using the metro, bus, or RER frequently during your stay, you may want to invest in a multi-day pass.

One of the best ways to learn about a Parisian culture is through its food, so do as the locals do and eat like a true foodie. Explore the neighbourhood cafes and eateries, and stop by the farmers market for some tasty snacks.

Take a walking tour: Exploring a new city on foot is one of the best ways to get to know it, and Paris is a beautiful place to do just that.

A walking tour is the best option to get to know a city and its culture and history. You may find numerous walking excursions in Paris that won't break the bank.

Change your mind. While having a strategy in place is helpful, it's also crucial to be adaptable and willing to make changes as needed. The city is full of unexpected treasures.

Adaptability and willingness to try new things are important because life doesn't always go as planned.

Even if tipping is not typical in France, Paris is an exception because of the large number of international visitors it receives each year. A donation of more than 10 per cent is greatly appreciated.

Stop and rest; don't try to accomplish too much in a single sitting. Spend some downtime soaking in the ambience at a nearby park or café.

If you want to avoid crowds and shorter waits, plan your trip for the shoulder seasons (spring and fall).

Eat at local restaurants, go to local events, and explore off-the-beaten-path neighbourhoods to immerse yourself in your destination's culture truly.

If you follow these tips, you will have a good time in Paris and bring home wonderful memories.

Have fun, and don't worry too much about following a precise agenda; instead, take time to appreciate the beauty and charm of Paris.

THE BEST WAYS TO SAVE MONEY IN PARIS

Saving money when in Paris is essential. However, many inexpensive ways exist to experience the city's art, sightseeing, and dining.

Here are some major ways to save money while in Paris:

To easily navigate the city, purchase a metro card and use the extensive (over 300 stops) Parisian Metro system. There is a price difference of 1.60 EUR between a carnet of 10 tickets and a carnet of 10 tickets for a single day (both are much cheaper than paying 1.90 EUR for an individual ticket). The ParisVisite day pass saves admission to several of the city's top attractions.

Plan a picnic and enjoy the many parks and gardens available. Eating cheaply and well in Paris is possible by shopping for food there. Take a picnic to the park with some bread, cheese, and meat from the supermarket. All have fun, and the cost is far less than dining.

More than seventy of Paris's top museums and attractions accept the Paris Museum Pass, a pre-paid card that grants entry. The 2-day pass costs 52 EUR, the 4-day pass is 66 EUR, and the 6-day pass is 78 EUR. Ideal for those who enjoy spending time in art galleries. Because of the high volume of visitors to the city's museums, prices will naturally be lower.

The Paris Pass is a more comprehensive version of the Paris Museum Pass and is a must-have for visitors with limited time in the city. Prices start at 109 EUR for a 2-day pass and go to 129 EUR for three days, 149 EUR for four days, and 169 EUR for 6-days. Over 75 top attractions are included, and there is a hop-on, hop-off bus tour (in addition to everything in the Paris Museum Pass).

Every month on the first Sunday, National Museums across the country offer free entrance to the general public. If you plan on going today, you could have to wait in huge lines and deal with many people.

If you're trying to save money on meals while in Paris, eating out for lunch could be a good option. While meals might be quite pricey, many restaurants offer a fixed lunch menu for 10–20 Euros, a significant discount.

Saving money when travelling can be accomplished most effectively by preparing your meals. Nowadays, visitors at most hotels, B&Bs, and hostels can use the on-site kitchen to prepare their meals. No place to cook? Pack a container and utensils and make salads and sandwiches to eat on the go.

It's easy to meet interesting people and learn about a new place using Couchsurfing or a similar app to find a local host. We have an active and cooperative group of people here.

When ordering water at a restaurant, your only free choice is tap water. If they try to sell you bottled water at a premium, tell them you already know it's safe to drink straight from the tap.

Since the water from the tap may be safely used, filling up a reusable container beforehand is an easy way to cut costs and decrease trash. I highly recommend LifeStraw since its water bottles have built-in filters that ensure clean, safe drinking water wherever you go. Water refill stations could be located throughout the city.

RECOMMENDATIONS FOR ITINERARIES BASED ON DIFFERENT INTERESTS AND TRAVEL STYLES

Here are some itinerary recommendations based on different interests and travel styles for making the most of your time in Paris:

First-Time Visitors:

Day 1: Visit iconic landmarks such as Notre Dame Cathedral, the Eiffel Tower, and the Louvre Museum.

Day 2: Explore the Sacré-Cœur Basilica, the bohemian Montmartre neighbourhood, and the Moulin Rouge.

Day 3: Stroll along the Seine River, visit the Musée d'Orsay, and shop in the trendy Le Marais district.

Art and Culture Lovers:

Day 1: Visit the Louvre Museum, home to famous artworks such as the Mona Lisa and Venus de Milo.

Day 2: Explore the Musée d'Orsay, known for its Impressionist and Post-Impressionist art.

Day 3: Discover the Centre Pompidou, a modern art museum, and the Palais Garnier, an ornate opera house.

Foodies:

Day 1: Indulge in Parisian pastry shops and cafés, such as Ladurée and Angelina.

Day 2: Visit the Saint-Germain-des-Prés neighbourhood, known for its cheese shops, wine bars, and cafes.

Day 3: Take a food tour, visit local markets, and try French specialities such as escargot, foie gras, and macarons.

Fashionistas:

Day 1: Shop in the chic boutiques of the Champs-Élysées and the Avenue Montaigne.

Day 2: Visit the Galeries Lafayette and Printemps department stores for luxury fashion brands.

Day 3: Explore the trendy Le Marais and Saint-Germain-des-Prés neighbourhoods for boutique fashion shops.

History Buffs:

Day 1: Visit the Palace of Versailles, symbolizing the French monarchy's opulence.

Day 2: Explore the medieval district of the Île de la Cité, including the Sainte-Chapelle and the Conciergerie.

Day 3: Discover the Paris Catacombs, the Père Lachaise Cemetery, and the Musée de l'Armée.

These itineraries are just suggestions, and you can always mix and match based on your interests and preferences. While out and about in the city, stop and soak in some of the local flavours.

TRAVEL ADVICE: HOW TO MAKE THE MOST OF YOUR TIME AND STAY OUT OF TROUBLE

Learn how to make the most of your time in Paris and avoid the typical problems visitors encounter by reading on.

Do some preliminary reading about the destination and list must-see attractions and activities. You may use your time better and avoid procrastination by following this advice.

If you want to get around Paris quickly and easily, I recommend using the city's excellent public transit system. Learn about the city's public transportation system (subway, bus, and bike) and enjoy a fresh perspective by exploring on two wheels.

While Paris is constantly bustling, peak tourist seasons may be overwhelming. You may avoid crowds and enjoy shorter lines by travelling during the off-season.

It would help if you got up early to make the most of your time and avoid the crowds that form later in the day at many of Paris' most popular attractions.

Paris can be exhausting, so take breaks when you need them. Following these tips, you can make the most of your trip and prevent fatigue.

Don't be scared to explore the local cuisine and drinks; Paris is famous for its incredible food and drink culture. Immersing oneself in the local culture is a great approach to getting the most out of a trip.

Treat locals and their customs respectfully; Paris is home to its traditions and culture. Following these guidelines will ensure you have a wonderful trip and don't upset anyone.

Even though most Parisians can communicate in English, brushing up on some basic phrases in the local language is always a good idea before your trip.

Seeing the city's well-known landmarks is a must, but you shouldn't miss out on Paris's hidden gems. The best way to immerse yourself in the local culture and visit the sights without fighting the crowds is to hire a private guide.

Although it is recommended that you pack as much into your trip as possible, remember to take some time off to relax and take in the sights and sounds of the city. Taking time to unwind in Paris, whether at a café, while taking a stroll in a park, or while people-watching, will help you get the most out of your visit.

CONCLUSION

There is a never-ending supply of new and exciting things to discover and do in Paris. Every kind of traveller can find something of interest in this city, be it one of its well-known landmarks, one of its lesser-known neighbourhoods, or one of its many hidden jewels.

You'll be able to make the most of your time in Paris and get a feel for the city as if you were a native if you follow these pointers and recommendations, which cover topics such as navigating the public transportation system, finding affordable lodging and dining options, avoiding crowds and cons, and exploring the city's art, culture, and fashion scenes.

If you put some thought into planning your trip and go into it with an open mind, you might have an experience that will fill you with memories you will hold dear for the rest of your life. You will be able to create an incredible experience with the help of this.

Made in United States
North Haven, CT
01 April 2023